Biarritz

Travel Guide

2024

Unveiling the Coastal Charms, Local Delights, and Insider Tips for an Unforgettable Journey through the Basque Beauty

Emily Catlett

EMILY CATLETT

MAP OF BIARRITZ

SCAN THIS CODE TO ACCESS THE MAP

EMILY CATLETT

EMILY CATLETT

TABLE OF CONTENTS

INTRODUCTION

Biarritz is a jewel of the Basque coast, a shelter for those who are looking for both the comfort of nature and the thrill of adventure. It is located in the golden embrace of the Atlantic Ocean, where the waves whisper tales of ancient mariners and current surfers dance atop their crests. It was here, amid the combination of craggy cliffs and magnificent homes, which I discovered a narrative that was demanding to be told. Not through the perspective of a mere tourist, but with the closeness of a local, a wanderer who has walked its streets, breathed its air, and been entranced by its turquoise horizons.

This guidebook is the result of a series of moments, each of which will serve as a stroke of the brush in the colorful tapestry that is Biarritz. This book is more than just a travel guide; it is a companion for those who are pulled to this particular region of the world because they are curious, adventurous, and dreamers.

You will find hidden jewels buried away in cobbled roads, cafes where the aroma of freshly brewed coffee blends with the salty sea breeze, and secluded areas where the sunset paints the sky in shades of fire and gold. All of these discoveries will be made possible via my eyes.

Not only will you be traveling through the streets of Biarritz, but you will also be traveling through the city's essence. The enchantment that occurs when you travel freely through a city and allow it to show itself in its own time and manner is demonstrated by this guide, which is a monument to that magic. The purpose of this collection is to provide you, dear tourist, with a compilation of personal experiences, practical tips, and cultural insights that will assist you in creating your remarkable narrative while you are in Biarritz.

So pack your luggage, bring your sense of wonder, and let this book be your guide to the magical world of Biarritz. Discovering, experiencing, and appreciating the beauty of a location where every street, every wave, and every breeze has a tale to tell will be something that we together will do. As seen through my eyes, I would like to welcome you to Biarritz.

HISTORY AND CULTURE

The story of Biarritz originates in the early middle Ages when it was only a little community dedicated to whaling. Its strategic location near the Bay of Biscay made it a perfect spot for the Basque sailors to start on their risky hunts. However, it wasn't until the 19th century that Biarritz began to sparkle on the world stage, thanks to the patronage of the European aristocracy. Napoleon III and his wife, Eugénie, were among the first to disclose the potential of Biarritz as a beach resort. They built a magnificent summer mansion on the beach, which is today the iconic Hôtel du Palais, capturing the attention of aristocrats and wealthy guests from across Europe. The city immediately became linked with luxury and relaxation, a reputation it retains to this day.

But Biarritz is not just about its aristocratic history. It is also recognized as the surf capital of Europe. The sport was introduced here in the late 1950s by visiting American surfers, and since then, the city has been a crucial center for surf culture in Europe. The Côte des Basques beach, with its long, rolling waves, provides the perfect canvas for both novice and professional surfers. The annual Biarritz Surf Festival has grown to become one of the most major meetings for surf fans worldwide, celebrating not just the sport but also the laid-back, inclusive lifestyle that surrounds it.

The culture of Biarritz is heavily impacted by the Basque history, a proud and old population noted for its distinct language, culinary traditions, and folkloric music and dance. Visitors to Biarritz may enjoy the rich Basque culture through its food, which is a savory blend of sea and farm produce. Dishes like marmitako (tuna stew) and pintxos (small nibbles akin to tapas) are local favorites, delivering a glimpse of the region's gastronomic wealth. The city also hosts different events throughout the year that feature Basque music, dancing, and sports, offering a glimpse into the continuing traditions of this unique ethnic community.

Moreover, Biarritz has played its part on the world stage, hosting key diplomatic gatherings and summits. Its magnificent beaches and elegant hotels have offered a stunning backdrop for debates and accords that have formed the contemporary world. This blend of natural beauty, historical significance, and cultural depth makes Biarritz a unique site where the past and present merge perfectly, giving something for everyone.

WHY VISIT BRIARRITZ

1. Surf's Up: Biarritz is recognized as Europe's surf capital. Its beaches, such as the famous Côte des Basques, offer waves for surfers of every skill level. Whether you're looking to catch your first wave or searching for an adrenaline-filled ride, Biarritz's surf scene does not disappoint. Surf schools dot the beach, ready to educate newbies about the sport or help expert surfers refine their talents.

2. Cultural Richness: Beyond the beaches, Biarritz is a cultural treasure trove. The town's past as a luxury vacation for the European elite has left a legacy of spectacular buildings, including the grandiose Hôtel du Palais and the Russian Orthodox Church, with its characteristic blue dome. The town's museums, such as the Musée de la Mer, give a thorough dive into the marine life and local history, allowing an insight into the town's past and present.

3. Gastronomic Delights: French cuisine requires no introduction, and Biarritz is a testimony to this gastronomic tradition. Fresh seafood is a staple, with local eateries serving up everything from

traditional Basque meals to contemporary fusion cuisine. Don't miss the chance to taste pintxos, the Basque Country's counterpart to tapas, excellent for a tasty snack as you explore the town.

4. Natural Beauty: Biarritz is not simply about the ocean. The town is surrounded by natural beauty, from the rocky coasts affording spectacular views of the Bay of Biscay to the tranquil parks and gardens within the town itself. A walk along the coast at sunset or a trek to the neighboring lighthouse offers a chance to reconnect with nature and enjoy a moment of serenity away from the hectic town core.

5. Warm Hospitality: The inhabitants of Biarritz are known for their warm welcome and friendly temperament. Visitors often find themselves enchanted by the inhabitants' openness to share stories, recommend hidden gems, or just offer directions. This welcoming attitude makes it easy to feel at home in Biarritz, converting a simple visit into a memorable experience.

6. A Gateway to the Basque Country: Biarritz serves as the perfect starting place for visiting the larger Basque Country, an area rich in history, culture, and natural beauty. Whether you're interested in trekking in the Pyrenees, seeing little fishing villages, or discovering the dynamic city of San Sebastian just across the border in Spain, Biarritz gives easy access to these various activities.

EMILY CATLETT

CHAPTER 1

GETTING TO BIARRITZ

1. By Air

Flying into Biarritz is uncomplicated, with Biarritz Airport serving as the entryway to this charming town. Offering flights from numerous places across Europe, the airport connects tourists to the world with airlines that cater to a wide range of budgets and preferences. Once you land, the town is just a short ride away. You can select a taxi or a bus; both alternatives are available directly outside the terminal, enabling a hassle-free transfer from the air to the ground.

2. By Train

For those who like the scenic approach, traveling a train to Biarritz allows viewing the breathtaking scenery of the French countryside. The town's train station is well-connected, with frequent connections from large cities like Paris. The journey is not simply a means to an end but an experience in itself, exhibiting the beauty of France through the window of a luxurious train carriage.

3. By Road

Driving to Biarritz is another fantastic alternative for those wanting flexibility. The French road network is second to none, with well-maintained roadways going straight to the town. Whether you're hiring a car or driving your own, the drive is simple. Road signs are excellent, making navigating easier for people unfamiliar with the area. Plus, the drive down the coast gives stunning views of the Atlantic Ocean, making every moment behind the wheel an exciting part of your adventure.

4. By Bus

For the budget-conscious traveler, buses offer a cheap method to reach Biarritz. Various bus companies operate routes from key cities across France and Spain, providing a cost-effective choice without compromising on comfort. The bus journey is an opportunity to meet fellow travelers, swap tales, and soak in the scenery of rolling hills and bustling villages along the way.

CHAPTER 2

ACCOMMODATION OPTIONS

HOTELS

1. Hotel du Palais

Standing majestically by the Atlantic Ocean, the Hotel du Palais is not only a place to stay; it's a voyage into history. Once the summer residence of Napoleon III and Empress Eugenie, this hotel mixes imperial splendor with modern comfort. Its rooms and suites provide breathtaking ocean views, while the spa, swimming pool, and Michelin-starred restaurant cater to your every need. It's more than a hotel; it's an insight into the sumptuous lifestyle of French aristocracy.

2. Le Regina Biarritz Hotel & Spa

Overlooking the gorgeous Bay of Biscay, Le Regina Biarritz Hotel & Spa is the epitome of elegance. The hotel's unusual circular architecture, crowned with a magnificent glass dome, has elegantly designed rooms that merge contemporary flair with classic French grandeur. The spa, outdoor pool, and gourmet restaurant make it a refuge for relaxation and culinary delight.

3. Thalassa sea & spa at the Sofitel Biarritz Le Miramar

This hotel is a sanctuary for wellness enthusiasts. With immediate access to the beach, it provides a unique blend of Thalassotherapy treatments, an outdoor seawater pool, and a fitness center. The rooms and suites are designed for optimum comfort, with stunning views of the sea. The hotel's restaurants feature health-inspired cuisine that compliments the wellness experience.

4. Hotel Le Café de Paris

If you're lured to the center of Biarritz, Hotel Le Café de Paris offers an exceptional location. Situated in the lively city center, this hotel features accommodations with private balconies overlooking the ocean or the exciting city activity. The on-site restaurant offers a terrace with panoramic views, where you can taste native Basque cuisine and worldwide delicacies. It's the perfect position for people who want to be in the center of the action.

5. Radisson Blu Hotel, Biarritz

For visitors wanting a modern and sophisticated stay, the Radisson Blu Hotel is a wonderful alternative. Positioned close to the famed Côte des Basques beach, it offers a rooftop patio with a pool and spectacular views of the city and the sea. The contemporary accommodations, exercise facility, and choice of two restaurants provide a comfortable and convenient base for visiting Biarritz and its surroundings.

BED AND BREAKFASTS

1. The Coastal Retreat

This charming bed and breakfast is just a short walk from the famous Côte des Basques beach. It gives guests a friendly, family-like atmosphere in a traditional Basque house. The apartments are nicely adorned with local art and offer spectacular sea views. The proprietors are famed for their hospitality and serve a great, freshly prepared breakfast each morning. With only a handful of rooms, this facility ensures a tranquil and cozy stay, making it ideal for anyone wishing to unwind by the sea.

2. The Urban Oasis

Located in the center of Biarritz, our urban bed and breakfast offers a great blend of modern luxury and historic charm. Housed in a refurbished 19th-century structure, it boasts modern, contemporary rooms with all the conveniences you need for a comfortable stay. The highlight is the lovely garden where you may sip your morning coffee or unwind after a day of touring. The hosts are highly informed about the area and can provide fantastic ideas for meals and activities.

3. The Surfer's Haven

For those who travel to Biarritz for its famed waves, this bed & breakfast offers the ultimate surfer's hideaway. Situated next to some of the top surf places, it not only provides quick access to the beach but also offers surfboard storage and drying areas. The vibe is laid-back and sociable, with a shared lounge space excellent for meeting fellow visitors. Rooms are modest yet comfortable, with vivid details that represent the local surf culture.

4. The Garden Hideaway

This quaint bed & breakfast is a truly hidden gem, located in a quiet residential part of Biarritz. It features a magnificent garden where guests can rest among flowers and fruit trees. The rooms are nicely designed and feature plenty of natural light, providing a tranquil environment to unwind. The hosts pride themselves on utilizing organic and locally sourced products for their breakfast, which may be enjoyed on the patio overlooking the garden.

5. The Artistic Getaway

For those with a love for art and design, this bed and breakfast is a dream come true. Each apartment is distinctively furnished with pieces from local artists and designers, providing an inspiring and creative atmosphere. It's a bit further from the beach but offers a calm environment with wonderful views of the Biarritz countryside.

The hosts organize regular art exhibitions and seminars, allowing guests a chance to participate in the local art community.

VACATION RENTALS

1. Oceanfront Luxury Apartment

Imagine waking up to the relaxing sound of waves and the sight of the sunrise over the Atlantic. This stylish apartment delivers exactly that. With its huge sitting space, fully outfitted kitchen, and spectacular ocean views, it's great for individuals who prefer comfort and elegance. The great location enables quick access to the ocean, local markets, and trendy cafes, making it an ideal base for your explorations in Biarritz.

2. Charming Historic Villa

Step back in time with a stay at this beautifully renovated villa. Blending historical elegance with modern amenities, this property boasts magnificent woodwork, soaring ceilings, and a verdant garden. It's a short walk from the city's famous beaches and busy nightlife, offering a calm respite after a day of adventure. The property comfortably accommodates large parties or families, ensuring everyone has space to decompress.

3. Cozy Beachside Studio

Perfect for lone travelers or couples, this studio apartment combines comfort and convenience in a tiny setting. Located only feet from the beach, it's fitted with a comfy bed, a small kitchenette, and a private terrace. The studio's basic style and careful accents create a warm and friendly atmosphere. With easy access to surf schools and beachside eateries, it's a perfect alternative for those wishing to enjoy Biarritz's laid-back lifestyle.

4. Elegant Townhouse with Private Terrace

This townhouse blends the finest of city living with the peacefulness of a private home. The inside is elegantly furnished, offering a blend of traditional and contemporary elements. Guests can appreciate the vast living areas, a modern kitchen, and a quiet terrace great for outdoor dining or sunbathing. Located in the middle of Biarritz, it's just a short walk from the beach, shopping, and dining options, delivering an authentic experience of the city.

5. Secluded Garden Cottage

For a more private and quiet vacation, this home is a great alternative. Surrounded by a magnificent garden, it offers solitude and tranquility while being accessible to all that Biarritz has to offer. The cottage offers a nice bedroom, a living space with a fireplace, and a fully equipped kitchen. It's a romantic getaway for couples or a calm retreat for anybody wishing to unwind and rejuvenate.

CHAPTER 3

EXPLORING BIARRITZ

TOP ATTRACTIONS

The Great Beach (Grande Plage) is a must-visit for anyone going to Biarritz. This beach is not simply a place to soak up the sun; it's a living postcard of the city's dynamic energy. With its golden beaches stretching beneath the watchful eye of the renowned Hotel du Palais, the beach offers both relaxation and an insight into the luxury side of Biarritz's history. Surfers and sunbathers both find a sanctuary here, making it an ideal site for both adventure and pleasure.

No visit to Biarritz is complete without seeing the Rock of the Virgin (Rocher de la Vierge). This natural monument, accessible by a metal bridge created by Gustave Eiffel, offers stunning views of the Atlantic Ocean. The rock itself, with a statue of the Virgin Mary standing guard, is a testimony to the city's marine tradition and provides a unique vantage point for watching the sunset.

The Biarritz Lighthouse, rising tall at the northernmost point of the city, gives another panoramic perspective of the Basque coast. A hike to the top rewards visitors with a wide view of Biarritz and its surroundings, from the beaches to the Pyrenees Mountains. The lighthouse is not merely a signal for ships; it's a symbol of the city's continuous relationship to the sea.

The City of the Ocean (Cité de l'Océan), a museum dedicated to the ocean and its wonders, is an educational landmark in Biarritz. Through interactive exhibits and fascinating installations, visitors of all ages may learn about marine life, oceanography, and the need to maintain our seas. This attraction mixes fun with learning, making it great for families.

Biarritz's old Market Hall (Les Halles de Biarritz) is a culinary delight. This lively market is where locals and visitors alike gather to experience and buy the best local fruit, meats, cheeses, and more. The neighboring taverns and restaurants offer a chance to try Basque cuisine, making the Market Hall a focal point for food aficionados.

For a touch of luxury and history, the Imperial Chapel (Chapelle Impériale) is a sight to behold. Built for Empress Eugenie in the 19th century, this chapel is a remarkable blend of neo-Gothic and neo-Byzantine architecture. Its tranquil ambiance and detailed decorations make it a peaceful getaway from the city's hustle and bustle.

Lastly, the Biarritz Aquarium, set on the cliffs overlooking the Bay of Biscay, immerses visitors in the aquatic world. With its collection of local and tropical fish, sharks, and seals, the aquarium is a fantastic site for marine life enthusiasts. The view of the sea from the aquarium adds to the enchanting experience.

BEACHES

First on the list is the Grande Plage, the main beach of Biarritz, noted for its large stretch of golden sand and bustling environment. It's a location where families congregate, friends meet, and the spirit of summer is alive all year round. The ocean here welcomes swimmers and surfers alike to confront its waves, delivering a thrill for daring and fun for those wishing to dip their toes in the water.

For those seeking a quieter hideaway, the Côte des Basques is a must-visit. This beach is a sanctuary for surfers, providing waves that appeal to all levels of ability. The view from the seashore, with the rocky cliffs and the Spanish coast in the distance, is simply breathtaking. It's a fantastic site for a tranquil day spent riding waves or relaxing on the sand, letting the ocean's cadence soothe your spirit.

Plage du Port Vieux gives a different kind of appeal. Sheltered by rocks, this modest beach feels like a hidden paradise in the middle of Biarritz. Its tranquil seas make it suitable for families and individuals who prefer a more sheltered setting for swimming. The spirit of camaraderie here is obvious, with locals and visitors alike sharing in the simple joy of a day at the beach.

For a touch of luxury and a glimpse into Biarritz's dazzling past, travel to Plage Miramar. This beach, near the renowned Hôtel du Palais, is less busy and emanates a sense of luxury and quiet. It's a lovely spot to unwind, with the big ocean in front of you and the splendor of Biarritz's belle époque behind.

Lastly, Milady Beach has something for everyone. With its playground for children, accessible paths, and dynamic surf scene, it's a location where every visitor may find their slice of happiness. The beach is also a starting point for spectacular coastal hikes, encouraging you to experience the natural beauty of the Basque coast beyond the sand.

MUSEUMS AND GALLERIES

1. The Asiatica Museum

This museum is a must-visit for anyone interested in Eastern art. It holds one of the most extensive collections of Asian art in France, containing pieces from India, Nepal, Tibet, and China. The meticulously curated displays provide a deep dive into the art, culture, and history of these regions. Walking through the museum is like taking a voyage through Asia, with each piece conveying its tale.

2. The Historical Museum of Biarritz

Located in a former Anglican church, this museum offers a unique peek into Biarritz's past. It covers the chronology of the city from its fishing hamlet roots to being a favorite holiday resort for European nobility and celebrities. The collection comprises images, relics, and models that bring the history of Biarritz to life. It's a terrific spot to study how this city evolved into the popular resort it is now.

3. The Sea Museum

For ocean lovers, the Sea Museum is an intriguing stop. It's not just a museum; it's an aquatic journey, showing the marine life of the Bay of Biscay and beyond. With its aquariums, seals, and sharks, it offers an instructive yet exhilarating experience for all ages. The museum also digs into the history of fishing and whaling in the region, demonstrating the relationship between Biarritz and the sea.

4. Art Galleries

Biarritz is home to various art galleries that highlight modern art. These places are where local and foreign artists display their work, ranging from paintings and sculptures to digital art. Visiting these galleries, you'll get a taste of the active artistic scene of Biarritz. Each gallery has its unique flair, presenting a fresh viewpoint on modern art.

PARKS AND GARDENS

1. The Public Garden (Jardin Public de Biarritz)

This old garden is a nice setting for a quiet walk or a relaxed retreat. With its wide roads lined with diverse trees and flowers, it creates a cool, shaded location excellent for those sunny days. The garden is well-maintained, including traditional French landscaping, and it's a favorite place for both locals and tourists. It's a great spot for reading a book, enjoying a leisurely lunch, or simply soaking up the tranquil ambiance.

2. Lake Marion

A bit off the usual road, Lake Marion is a hidden treasure for anyone wishing to escape the rush and bustle of the city. This natural lake is surrounded by a thick forest, offering a choice of walking trails that are perfect for families and environment enthusiasts. The area is filled with animals, and the serene settings make it an ideal site for bird viewing or a tranquil walk.

3. Miremont Tea Garden

For those who love a side of history with their nature hikes, the Miremont Tea Garden is a delightful stop. Located near the famed Miremont patisserie, this park offers beautiful views of the ocean and the Grande Plage. It's a nice area to rest after seeing the city or to have a delicious treat from the bakery. The mix of breathtaking views and great flavors makes this garden a unique experience in Biarritz.

4. Villa Belza's Gardens

Perched on the cliffs overlooking the Côte des Basques, the gardens of Villa Belza are not commonly known but are certainly a pleasure to behold. The villa itself is an iconic property with a rich history, and its gardens give stunning views of the sea and the surrounding coastline. It's a bit of a climb to get there, but the panoramic views and the quiet garden setting are well worth the effort.

5. Plaza Berri

Plaza Berri is a modern park in the middle of Biarritz, offering a green refuge within the urban landscape. It's a terrific location for youngsters to play, with plenty of open space and sophisticated play equipment. The park also incorporates contemporary artworks, bringing an artistic touch to the natural settings. It's a fantastic illustration of how Biarritz merges the traditional with the modern, creating places that are both beautiful and efficient.

CHAPTER 4

OUTDOOR ACTIVITIES

SURFING

Why Biarritz Stands Out for Surfing

Biarritz's reputation as Europe's surf capital isn't just hype. The city boasts multiple beaches, each giving distinct conditions appropriate for surfers of all skill levels. Grande Plage, the major beach, is excellent for beginners and intermediate surfers, while Côte des Basques, recognized as the cradle of surfing in France, delivers more demanding waves for the expert. Beyond the waves, Biarritz's surf culture is apparent, with multiple surf schools, shops, and events that cater to the surf community.

1. Best Time to Surf in Biarritz

While Biarritz offers outstanding surfing conditions year-round, the best waves typically roll in from late spring to early fall (May to October). During these months, the weather is warm, and the Atlantic Ocean offers steady swells. However, if you prefer quieter times, consider going in the shoulder season's spring or fall when the tourists thin out but the surf remains steady.

2. Surfing Lessons and Equipment

For those wishing to acquire or perfect their surfing talents, Biarritz boasts lots of surf schools offering training for all ages and levels. These schools provide not just training but also all the essential equipment, making it easy for vacationers to hit the waves without the burden of packing their gear. Renting surfboards and wetsuits is also an option for individuals who want to venture out on their own.

3. A Few Tips for Your Surf Trip

Respect the ocean and local surf etiquette. Understanding the right of way and keeping the beaches clean ensures a great experience for everyone.

Stay flexible with your surf plans. Ocean conditions can change, so be open to exploring various areas or even enjoying other activities Biarritz has to offer on no-surf days.

Connect with the local surf community. Visiting local surf shops and cafes or attending surf competitions can improve your trip and provide vital insights into the finest places and conditions.

EMILY CATLETT

GOLFING

Why Biarritz Stands Out for Golfers

Biarritz shines as a golfing location for various reasons. The town's environment is mild year-round, making it a perfect site for golf no matter the season. The diversity of courses surrounding Biarritz accommodates all skill levels, from beginners to seasoned pros. Whether you're hoping to challenge your talents on a championship course or enjoy a leisurely round with spectacular ocean views, Biarritz has something special to offer.

1. Top Golf Courses to Visit

Le Phare Golf Course: Located in the center of Biarritz, Le Phare is one of the oldest and most regarded courses in the area. Its relatively level topography gives a good challenge without being overly difficult, great for a relaxing game.

Ilbarritz Training Center: Just a short drive from the town center, Ilbarritz is unique. It's not simply a course but a whole training facility situated against an ocean setting. It's perfect for sharpening your talents.

Chiberta Golf Course: A mix of links and forest, Chiberta is noted for its beauty as much as for its difficulties. The track runs beside the beaches and through pine forests, giving various scenery.

2. Making the Most of Your Golfing Trip

Booking Tee Times: It's advisable to book your rounds in advance, especially during the summer months when courses may get busy. Most clubs provide online reservations, making it easier to manage your itinerary.

Beyond Golf: While golf could be the focus of your trip, Biarritz's rich culture, superb cuisine, and lovely beaches should not be overlooked. Take time to explore the area, taste the local food, and maybe even catch a wave at one of the famous surfing sites.

HIKING AND BIKING

1. Biking Adventures

The city and its surroundings cater to bikers of all levels. Whether you're renting a bike for a relaxing ride along the beach or exerting yourself on the mountainous paths outside the city, Biarritz serves as a great base. Key routes include:

The Coastal Path: This accessible route offers spectacular ocean vistas and breezes, linking Biarritz to other beaches and villages. Ideal for a family outing or a comfortable solitary ride.

The Countryside Trails: For those seeking more of a challenge, the rolling hills and attractive villages further inland provide enough options for exploring. These roads give a glimpse into the Basque Country's pastoral charm.

2. Hiking Trails

On foot, the landscapes of Biarritz emerge in astonishing richness. From cliffside walkways to woodland trails, hikers can find both easy walks and more strenuous hikes within reach.

La Rhune Mountain: For a full-day climb, La Rhune offers pathways that lead to the top of one of the region's most prominent peaks, rewarding hikers with stunning views across France and Spain.

The Coastal Walk: A less difficult choice, this path stretches along the sea, allowing easy access to Biarritz's beaches and secret coves, great for a rest or a swim.

3. Planning Your Adventure

Before venturing out, a bit of planning may ensure a smooth encounter. Bike rentals are offered throughout Biarritz, offering anything from mountain bikes to electric bikes. For trekking, it's recommended to check the weather, wear appropriate footwear, and take water, especially during the warmer months.

Local Insights

Engaging with locals or visiting the tourism office can unearth lesser-known paths and recommendations, enriching your journey.

Local markets also give the option to sample regional items, suitable for a picnic along your trip.

Safety and Respect

While enjoying the great outdoors, remember to respect trail signs, stay on established trails to conserve the environment, and be cautious of weather conditions. Additionally, sharing the routes politely with fellow adventurers promotes a great experience for everybody.

CHAPTER 5

DINING AND NIGHTLIFE

LOCAL CUISINE

At the heart of Biarritz's culinary scene are the fresh, high-quality ingredients acquired from both the sea and the land. Seafood aficionados will enjoy the number of alternatives available. The Atlantic Ocean provides a variety of seafood and shellfish that are beautifully prepared in local restaurants. One must-try meal is the "marmitako," a substantial tuna stew that warms the spirit and highlights the simplicity and depth of Basque cookery.

Another cornerstone of the local cuisine is the famous "pintxos," little snacks that deliver a punch of flavor. These Basque area staples are more than just cuisine; they represent a way of life. Strolling through the markets and restaurants of Biarritz, you'll see a diversity of pintxos, from skewered shellfish to small copies of traditional cuisine. It's a fantastic opportunity to try a range of local delicacies without committing to a full meal.

Cheese connoisseurs will find themselves in heaven in Biarritz. The region is home to the Ossau-Iraty, a creamy, nutty sheep's milk cheese that is commonly eaten with cherry jam or honey. It's a beautiful combination of sweet and savory that symbolizes the pastoral splendor of the Basque countryside.

No gastronomic excursion to Biarritz would be complete without plunging into the realm of Basque cakes and pastries. The "gateau Basque" is undoubtedly the most iconic, a soft, buttery cake filled with black cherry jam or pastry cream. Enjoying a slice of this cake at a local café, possibly with a view of the ocean, is one of life's simple joys.

Beyond the dishes themselves, what makes eating in Biarritz so remarkable is the warmth and hospitality of the residents. Restaurants and bistros frequently feel like extensions of someone's home, where cooks take pleasure in their art and are eager to tell the tales behind their food. It's this connection between food, place, and people that raise the experience from merely eating to truly appreciating.

RESTAURANTS AND CAFES

1. Le Clos Basque

Situated a short stroll from the famed Grande Plage, Le Clos Basque is a real gem that offers a comfortable eating experience. This restaurant is recognized for its adherence to Basque culinary traditions, serving meals that highlight the region's rich flavors and fresh ingredients. From exquisite seafood to robust beef dishes, each meal is a testament to the chef's expertise and the local produce's quality.

2. Café du Commerce

Located in the bustling heart of Biarritz, Café du Commerce is an iconic location that marries the charm of a classic French bistro with the laid-back ambiance of a coastal town. Whether you're searching for a location to have a leisurely breakfast or a seat to appreciate a glass of wine as the day winds down, this cafe has it all. Its cuisine comprises a range of French classics, with a specific emphasis on seafood.

3. Chez Albert

For those seeking an unmatched seafood experience, Chez Albert is the place to go. Nestled by the historic port, this restaurant offers spectacular views of the sea, complementing its superb seafood dishes. The setting is as enticing as the meal, with a nautical motif that pays respect to Biarritz's marine heritage. The fresh fish of the day served with a bit of Basque flair, is a must-try.

4. La Humade

If you're seeking traditional Basque cuisine, La Humade will not disappoint. This quaint café, tucked away in a quieter section of town, is recognized for its welcoming environment and scrumptious food. From classic pintxos (little appetizers) to powerful stews, the cuisine is a celebration of local culinary traditions. Dining here delivers not simply a meal, but a comprehensive dive into Basque culture.

5. Le Surfing

Overlooking the Côte des Basques, one of Biarritz's most famous surf areas, Le Surfing offers a unique dining experience that blends superb food with beautiful views. The menu is a creative blend of French and foreign cuisine, suitable for anyone looking to experience something new. Its laid-back environment makes it a great setting for a relaxed supper after a day of surfing or touring the area.

6. Miremont

Established in 1872, Miremont is a classic patisserie and tea restaurant that enjoys panoramic views of the Grande Plage. This classy business is great for anyone wishing to enjoy a sweet treat or a quiet afternoon tea. The pastries are nothing short of magnificent marvels, each telling a narrative of tradition and workmanship.

7. 100 Marches

Named for the surrounding steps that lead down to one of Biarritz's most beautiful beaches, 100 Marches is a bustling bar and restaurant that comes alive as the sun sets. It's the perfect area to enjoy a cocktail or a light dinner while soaking up the beautiful seaside views. The atmosphere is electrifying, with live music and DJ sets adding to the energetic vibe.

BARS AND NIGHTCLUBS

1. Le Surfing

Located close to the Côte des Basques, this pub offers a relaxing ambiance with spectacular ocean views. It's the perfect position for individuals who want to watch the sunset with a glass in hand. The attitude here is laid-back, echoing the surfing culture Biarritz is known for. Address: 9 Boulevard du Prince de Galles, Biarritz.

2. Le Caveau

This nightclub is a fixture for locals and visitors alike, recognized for its energetic atmosphere and broad music selection. From electronic sounds to chart-toppers, Le Caveau keeps the party going into the early hours. It's situated in the middle of Biarritz, giving it a convenient stop for a night out. Address: 4 Rue Gambetta, Biarritz.

3. Bar de la Côte

Overlooking the Port Vieux beach, this pub is known for its pleasant setting and outstanding assortment of wines and cocktails. It's a nice place to rest after a day of visiting Biarritz. The outdoor seating allows you to enjoy the sea air as you sip on your drink. Address: 8 Rue Port Vieux, Biarritz.

4. The Arena Biarritz

For those who appreciate live music and DJ sets, The Arena Biarritz is the go-to venue. It features a range of events from rock concerts to electronic evenings. The vast dance floor and state-of-the-art sound equipment combine for an amazing night out. Address: 15 Avenue Edouard VII, Biarritz.

5. Le Royale

A sophisticated bar that attracts a fashionable audience, Le Royale offers a selection of inventive cocktails and slick, modern decor. It's the place to be seen and to have a stylish night out in Biarritz. The bartenders are famed for their mixology talents, so don't hesitate to try something new here. Address: 8 Avenue de la Reine Victoria, Biarritz.

6. Hemingway's Café

Named after the great author, this café evolves into a lively bar as the night advances. It boasts a pleasant, inviting environment with a superb assortment of beers and spirits. Hemingway's is great for anyone wishing to spend a quiet evening in a place with charm. Address: 5 Rue Jean Bart, Biarritz.

7. Le Club

If you're into elite nightlife experiences, Le Club is where you want to be. Known for its VIP service and premium environment, this nightclub promises a sumptuous night out. With a tight dress code and a selection of premium cocktails, it's a place to enjoy the high life in Biarritz. Address: 22 Rue Gardères, Biarritz.

CHAPTER 6

SHOPPING

LOCAL MARKETS

When you visit Biarritz, you'll discover that each market has its unique charm, offering an insight into the local lifestyle and traditions. The primary marketplaces to explore include the Halles de Biarritz, an essential trip for food aficionados. Here, the stalls overflow with the freshest produce from the region, from dazzling fish taken just offshore to an array of cheeses, meats, and artisan bread that highlight the gastronomic diversity of the Basque country. It's not simply a location to buy your groceries; it's where folks socialize, swap news, and enjoy the simple pleasure of selecting the best ingredients for their meals.

Another highlight is the open-air market at Place des Cinq Cantons. This market comes alive with sellers offering everything from fresh fruits and vegetables to homemade crafts and garments. The atmosphere is lively, and the sense of camaraderie is obvious. It's a spot to sit down and absorb the moment, perhaps with a freshly made coffee from one of the neighboring cafés as you watch the world go by.

For those with a love for vintage discoveries and unique souvenirs, the Brocante Market is a must-visit. Held on select days at the Halles region, this market provides an eclectic variety of items, from antique furniture and vintage apparel to books and collectibles. It's a treasure trove for collectors and a great way to spend a morning or afternoon.

Visiting these markets is more than simply a shopping expedition; it's an opportunity to connect with the local culture. You'll meet the sellers who take pleasure in their items, each with a story to tell about their wares. It's an opportunity to practice your French, sample goods you've never had before, and take home a piece of Biarritz that goes beyond the usual tourist gifts.

Beyond the actual products you may buy, the markets of Biarritz offer a deeper sense of the town's rhythm and soul. The lively exchanges, the rich aromas of preparing food, and the vivid displays create a sensory experience that enriches your stay and leaves you with lasting memories.

BOUTIQUES AND SHOPS

1. Rue Mazagran

Start your shopping journey in Rue Mazagran, where modest boutiques line the cobblestone streets. From trendy couture to handcrafted jewelry, you'll find something to fit every taste.

2. Les Halles

Dive into the vivid ambiance of Les Halles, Biarritz's busy indoor market. Here, you may enjoy local delicacies including freshly caught fish, handcrafted cheeses, and aromatic spices. Don't forget to pick up a bottle of Basque cider or a jar of peppery Espelette pepper to take home with you.

3. Place Clemenceau

Wander down to Place Clemenceau, the hub of Biarritz's commercial district. Browse designer boutiques and premium department stores, or have a café au lait at one of the quaint sidewalk cafes while watching the world go by.

4. Port Vieux

For a taste of beach beauty, head to Port Vieux, where colorful fishing boats bob in the port. Explore the unique mix of businesses selling beachwear, surf gear, and artisanal goods. Be sure to sample the local specialties, like creamy Basque sheep's cheese and flaky pastries loaded with cherry jams.

5. Avenue Edouard VII

Stroll down Avenue Edouard VII, a tree-lined promenade studded with upmarket boutiques and art galleries. Admire the Belle Époque architecture as you shop for premium apparel brands and one-of-a-kind gifts.

6. Saint Charles

Discover the hidden gems of Saint Charles, a lovely district famed for its artisan workshops and independent retailers. Lose yourself in the maze of little alleyways lined with colorful facades, where you'll find anything from handcrafted pottery to vintage treasures.

7. La Négresse

Escape the rush and bustle of the city center and explore La Négresse, a calm suburb tucked between the ocean and the pine forests. Browse boho boutiques and eccentric surf stores, or relax on the sandy shores of Miramar Beach.

CHAPTER 7

DAY TRIP FROM BIARRITZ

SAN SEBASTIAN, SPAIN

1. Getting There

Hop in your car or board a bus for the picturesque ride from Biarritz to San Sebastian. The drive takes just about an hour, meandering through magnificent scenery and along the craggy coastline. Alternatively, go for a train journey for a hassle-free commute with spectacular vistas along the way.

2. Explore the Old Town

Step into the heart of San Sebastian by experiencing its historic Old Town, known as Parte Vieja. Lose yourself in the maze of narrow lanes dotted with colorful architecture, buzzing pintxo bars, and boutique shops. Take your time to roam and take in the colorful atmosphere.

3. Indulge in Pintxos

No visit to San Sebastian is complete without indulging in pintxos, the city's famous Basque-style tapas. Head to one of the many bars in the Old Town and experience a selection of wonderful meals, from freshly cooked fish to exquisite cured meats. Don't forget to combine your pintxos with a drink of local Txakoli wine or a cool Basque cider.

4. Relax on La Concha Beach

After seeing the Old Town, unwind on the golden sands of La Concha Beach. With its tranquil seas and breathtaking views of Santa Clara Island, it's the perfect area to soak up the sun or take a refreshing plunge in the sea. Grab a towel and pick a nice area to rest, or wander down the promenade and view the magnificent panoramas.

5. Visit Mount Urgull

For magnificent views of San Sebastian and the surrounding beaches, trek atop Mount Urgull. Located near the fringe of the Old Town, this picturesque hill offers stunning panoramas from its summit. Follow the twisting pathways through lush foliage and old defenses, and be rewarded with breathtaking views of the city below.

6. Discover Basque Culture

Take some time to immerse yourself in Basque culture during your vacation to San Sebastian. Visit the San Telmo Museum to learn about the region's rich history and legacy, or see a traditional Basque dance performance at one of the city's cultural institutions. Don't forget to sample some Basque delicacies, including creamy Idiazabal cheese or rich Tarta de Santiago almond cake.

7. Sunset at Monte Igueldo

End your day journey with a magnificent sunset from Monte Igueldo. Take the funicular railway to the summit, where you'll be treated to stunning views of the sun lowering beyond the horizon. Capture the occasion with a photo or simply sit back and soak in the splendor of the evening sky.

BAYONNE

Start your day with a stroll around the historic Old Town, where tiny cobblestone alleyways snake their way past centuries-old buildings embellished with colorful shutters. As you roam, take in the sights and sounds of local life, from the perfume of freshly made bread drifting from traditional boulangeries to the lively chatter of people having a morning espresso at a sidewalk café.

No visit to Bayonne would be complete without sampling its famed chocolate. Renowned for its rich and velvety texture, Bayonne chocolate has been manufactured in the city since the 17th century. Head to one of the local chocolatiers to indulge in a sampling session, where you can experience an array of flavors ranging from basic dark chocolate to unique fruit-infused variants.

After feeding your sweet taste, make your way to the stately Cathédrale Sainte-Marie de Bayonne, a marvel of Gothic architecture that dominates the city skyline. Step inside to observe the soaring vaulted ceilings, elaborate stained glass windows, and ornate altars covered with gilded sculptures. Take time to breathe in the serene environment and wonder at the artistry of this centuries-old cathedral.

For lunch, why not taste some of the region's culinary delights at one of Bayonne's traditional Basque restaurants? From robust cassoulet stews to delicate seafood dishes, there's something to satisfy every appetite. Pair your meal with a glass of locally made wine or cider for the perfect gourmet experience.

After lunch, take a stroll along the banks of the River Nive, where you may see panoramic views of the city and its surrounding landscape. Cross the landmark Pont Saint-Esprit Bridge to explore the beautiful Petit Bayonne district, where you'll find a bustling mix of artisan boutiques, small galleries, and lively street markets.

As the afternoon draws to a close, why not indulge in a touch of shopping? Bayonne is home to a multitude of unique stores and boutiques providing everything from handcrafted pottery to locally produced cheeses. Pick up a keepsake to remind you of your day trip to this wonderful city.

As the sun begins to set, make your way back to Biarritz, taking one final lingering glance at the gorgeous streets of Bayonne.

SAINT-JEAN-DE-LUZ

Start your day with a stroll through the ancient center of Saint-Jean-de-Luz. Admire the lovely Basque architecture as you meander along cobblestone streets surrounded by colorful cottages. Stop by the Eglise Saint-Jean-Baptiste, a majestic church steeped in history and embellished with delicate woodwork.

After seeing the town center, travel to the bustling fish market along the harbor. Here, you can enjoy fresh seafood harvested that morning by local fishermen. Don't miss the chance to eat the region's specialty, "chipirones" (baby squid), grilled to perfection in garlic and olive oil.

For lunch, indulge in a classic Basque meal at one of the town's many eateries. Savor delicacies like "piperade" (a savory pepper and tomato stew) or "axoa" (a substantial veal stew) accompanied with a glass of locally-produced wine or cider.

After lunch, take a quiet stroll along the seaside promenade. Admire breathtaking views of the Atlantic Ocean and watch as surfers catch waves along the sandy beaches. If you're feeling daring, why not try your hand at surfing or paddleboarding?

For those interested in history, a visit to the Maison de l'Infante is a must. This 17th-century mansion was formerly home to the Infanta of Spain and offers insight into the town's regal past.

Nature aficionados will adore exploring the adjacent coastal trails that give beautiful views of the rough shoreline. Take a trek along the picturesque cliffs or rent a bike to explore the countryside at your speed.

Before heading back to Biarritz, be sure to pick yourself some souvenirs to remember your vacation by. Browse the local shops for handmade Basque crafts, including traditional ceramics, textiles, and jewelry.

CHAPTER 8

PRACTICAL INFORMATION

WEATHER AND CLIMATE

1. Seasons in Biarritz:

Spring: Springtime in Biarritz is a sight to behold, with nature coming alive in a rush of vivid colors. Temperatures begin to warm up, ranging from comfortable lows in the 50s Fahrenheit to pleasant highs in the 60s and 70s. It's the best time to explore the town's lovely streets and enjoy a stroll along the coastline.

Summer: As summer rolls in, Biarritz changes into a bustling beach paradise. With long, sunny days and temps hanging in the 70s and 80s, it's excellent beach weather. Whether you're soaking up the sun on one of Biarritz's sandy beaches or trying your hand at surfing in the legendary waves, summer here is pure delight.

Fall: Autumn provides a sense of peacefulness to Biarritz as crowds thin out, making it a great time for a peaceful escape. The weather stays warm, with temperatures gradually falling from the 70s to the 60s. It's a terrific season for outdoor activities like climbing in the neighboring hills or relishing superb local cuisine in one of Biarritz's quaint cafes.

Winter: Even in winter, Biarritz retains its attractiveness with a more laid-back vibe and spectacular seaside views. While temperatures may plunge into the 40s and 50s, it's still quite pleasant compared to other parts of Europe. Winter storms periodically roll in from the Atlantic, bringing soothing rainfall to the region and creating a pleasant setting for indoor activities like discovering Biarritz's rich history or indulging in spa treatments.

2. Climate Highlights:

Moderate Temperatures: Thanks to its coastal location, Biarritz has moderate temperatures year-round, making it a delightful trip no matter the season.

Oceanic Influence: The Bay of Biscay exerts a substantial influence on Biarritz's environment, cushioning excessive temperature changes and contributing to the town's mild weather patterns.

Rainfall Distribution: While rainfall is dispersed pretty equally throughout the year, the autumn and winter months tend to see significantly higher precipitation amounts. This precipitation supports the rich foliage that blankets Biarritz's landscape, adding to its natural splendor.

TRANSPORTATION

First and foremost, Biarritz is supplied by a reliable and comprehensive public transit system. Buses run frequently around the city, providing economical and easy transit to essential destinations such as beaches, commercial malls, and tourist attractions. With many bus routes spanning the city and nearby areas, getting around Biarritz couldn't be easier.

For those who prefer to travel on two wheels, Biarritz also offers a bike-sharing program. With multiple bike stations positioned around the city, riders may easily rent a bike and cycle their way around town. Not only is cycling a fun and eco-friendly way to explore Biarritz, but it also allows visitors to take in the sights and sounds of the city at their leisure.

Biarritz is well-equipped with taxi services, giving a speedy and simple choice for people who prefer door-to-door transportation. Taxis are easily available around the city and can be hailed on the street or hired in advance. Whether you're traveling to the airport, or train station, or simply need a lift to your next location, taxis offer a reliable and effective form of transportation in Biarritz.

For those wishing to explore the surrounding areas, Biarritz acts as a gateway to the greater Basque Country region. Rental car services are available in the city, allowing guests to venture out and see local cities, villages, and natural wonders at their speed. With well-maintained highways and scenic driving routes, renting a car allows the opportunity to explore the beauty of the Basque Country at leisure.

SAFETY TIPS

1. Be mindful of your surroundings

One of the most crucial safety guidelines when going to any new place is to be aware of your surroundings at all times. Biarritz is a lively city, and as a tourist, it might be easy to get lost in the fascinating beauty and colorful atmosphere. However, it is vital to keep attentive and pay attention to your surroundings to avoid any potential threats or scams.

2. Keep your valuables safe

Biarritz attracts a huge number of tourists, which regrettably also attracts pickpockets and burglars. To avoid being a victim of theft, always keep your valuables near to you and try to avoid carrying big sums of cash. It is also advisable to put your passport and other critical documents in a safe at your lodging.

3. Use official transportation

Biarritz has a well-connected and efficient public transit system, including buses and taxis. It is usually encouraged to use legitimate transportation options rather than hitchhiking or taking rides from strangers. If you plan on renting a car, make sure to educate yourself about the local traffic regulations and always follow them.

4. Know the emergency numbers

Before beginning your vacation to Biarritz, it is vital to jot down the emergency contact numbers for the local police, fire department, and ambulance service. In case of any emergency, you can rapidly call out for help and assistance.

5. Keep yourself hydrated and shield the light from your face.

Biarritz is famed for its gorgeous beaches, and you may spend a substantial amount of time outdoors under the sun. It is crucial to stay hydrated and avoid prolonged exposure to the sun to prevent heatstroke and sunburn. Always apply sunscreen and a hat to protect yourself from the sun's damaging rays.

6. Respect the ocean

The beaches in Biarritz are famous among surfers and swimmers, however it is vital to respect the ocean and be cautious when entering the sea. Pay attention to the caution flags and signage and never swim alone. If you are not an experienced surfer, it is essential to take instruction before attempting to ride the waves.

USEFUL PHRASES

1. Greetings:

"Bonjour" (bohn-zhoor) - Hello / Good morning

"Bonsoir" (bohn-swahr) - Good evening "Salut" (sah-loo) - Hi / Bye (informal)

2. Polite Expressions:

"S'il vous plaît" (seel voo pleh) - Please "Merci" (mehr-see) - Thank you

"Excusez-moi" (ehk-skew-zay mwah) - Excuse me

"Pardon" (pahr-dohn) - Sorry / Pardon me

3. Basic Interactions:

"Parlez-vous anglais?" (par-leh voo ahn-gleh) - Do you speak English?

"Je ne comprends pas" (zhuh nuh kohm-prahn pah) - I don't understand "Je suis désolé(e), je suis perdu(e)" (zhuh swee deh-zoh-leh, zhuh swee pehr-doo) - I'm sorry, I'm lost

4. Dining Out:

"Une table pour deux, s'il vous plaît" (ewn tah-bluh poor duh, seel voo pleh) - Kindly provide a table for two.

"L'addition, s'il vous plaît" (lah-dee-syon, seel voo pleh) - Please bring the bill.

"Délicieux!" (deh-lee-syuh) - Delicious!

"Encore du pain, s'il vous plaît" (ahn-kohr dyoo pahn, seel voo pleh) - More bread, please

5. Shopping:

"Combien ça coûte?" (kohm-byen sah koot) - How much does it cost?

"Je voudrais acheter ceci" (zhuh voo-dray ah-sheh-tey suh-see) - I would want to buy this "Avez-vous ceci en taille..." (ah-veh voo suh-see ahn tahy...) - Do you have this in size...

6. Directions:

"Où est la plage?" (oo eh lah plahzh) - What location is the beach?

"Tournez à gauche / droite" (toor-nay ah gohsh / drwaht) - Turn left / right

"C'est loin / près d'ici?" (seh lwa / preh dee-see) - Is it far / near from here?

7. Emergency Situations:

"Au secours!" (oh suh-koor) - Help!

"Appelez la police / une ambulance" (ah-peh-leh lah poh-lees / ewn ahm-byoo-lahns) - Call the police / an ambulance

"Je suis blessé(e)" (zhuh swee bleh-say) - I am injured

8. Expressing Gratitude:

"Merci beaucoup" (mehr-see boh-koo) - Thank you very much "C'est très gentil de votre part" (seh tray zhahn-teel duh voh-truh pahr) - That's extremely sweet of you "Je vous suis reconnaissant(e)" (zhuh voo swee ruh-koh-nay-sahn) - I am grateful to you

CONCLUSION

As we near the conclusion of our Biarritz travel guide for 2024, it's apparent that this seaside treasure on the Basque coast has a plethora of joys for visitors of all types. From its magnificent beaches and world-class surfing locations to its rich history, lively culture, and wonderful food, Biarritz delivers a unique experience that remains long after you've gone home.

Throughout this book, we've explored the captivating beauty of Biarritz, from its renowned attractions like the Rocher de la Vierge to its hidden jewels nestled away in small districts. We've looked into the region's intriguing history, from its modest origins as a fishing hamlet to its emergence as a fashionable vacation town preferred by the European aristocracy. We've experienced the delights of Basque cuisine, from delectable pintxos to freshly caught seafood, and found the bustling arts and cultural scene that continues to fascinate people from across the globe.

But beyond its visible charms, Biarritz provides something more profound a feeling of retreat, renewal, and connection with nature and oneself. Whether you're seeking excitement on the waves, leisure on the coast, or just a moment of tranquility among stunning scenery, Biarritz urges you to slow down, absorb the moment, and feel the magic of this intriguing location.

Now, when you ponder your next trip journey, let Biarritz call you with its seductive attraction. Take the plunge into its blue seas, meander through its picturesque alleys, and immerse yourself in the warmth of its inviting culture. Whether you're a seasoned traveler or starting on your first overseas vacation, Biarritz offers an experience unlike any other a voyage of exploration, inspiration, and memorable memories.

So, dear reader, when you close the pages of this book, I encourage you to take the next step and convert your dreams of Biarritz into reality. Let its beauty, its energy, and its boundless potential grab your heart and kindle your sense of wanderlust. Pack your luggage, book your ticket, and go on the journey of a lifetime Biarritz awaits, eager to fascinate, delight, and leave you enthralled.

Bon voyage, and may your trip to Biarritz be full of pleasure, amazement, and numerous moments of pure delight. Until we meet again on the sands of this wonderful resort, remember adventure is beckoning, and Biarritz is ready to greet you with open arms.

Are you ready to experience the charm of Biarritz for yourself? Book your trip now and go on a memorable adventure to one of the most intriguing locations on earth. Don't let this chance pass you by Biarritz is beckoning, and your adventure awaits.

Printed in Great Britain
by Amazon

40671249R00037